Inward Foreign Investments in India and China

A Comparative Perspective

Bibek Ray Chaudhuri

Institute of Foreign Policy Studies (IFPS)

Centre for Pakistan and West Asian Studies (CPWAS)

Calcutta University
Kolkata

KNOWLEDGE WORLD

KW Publishers Pvt Ltd
New Delhi

2011 FPBA BEST PUBLISHERS AWARD (ENGLISH)

The Court of Directors of the East India Company sent a despatch in July, 1854 to the Governor-General of India in Council, suggesting the establishment of the Universities of Calcutta, Madras and Bombay. In pursuance of that despatch, the University of Calcutta was founded on January 24, 1857. The University adopted in the first instance, the pattern of the University of London and gradually introduced modifications in its constitution.

The Institute of Foreign Policy Studies (IFPS) at the University of Calcutta is an autonomous centre devised for the study of international relations, with particular emphasis on foreign policy. Funded by the Ministry of External Affairs (MEA), Government of India, the institute purports to create a pool of foreign policy specialists capable of offering advice on matters pertaining to India's international relations. The Institute has already been earmarked for developing national expertise with reference to the Government of India's Look East Policy, and that towards West Asia. The IFPS has also been chosen as one of the ten centres for United Nations Academic Initiative, functioning as the hub for studies on peace and conflict resolution.

The Centre for Pakistan and West Asian Studies, Calcutta University, was set up in 2005 under the UGC Area Studies Programme. It is the only research outfit associated with a University in eastern India with an exclusive focus on Pakistan and West Asian countries, Afghanistan, Iran and Iraq in particular, which together constitute a part of India's extended neighbourhood in the West. The Centre, since its establishment in 2005, has tried to develop a greater understanding of this extended neighbourhood by looking at the internal dynamics of the region with far greater detail than is generally accorded by other area studies outfits in the country.

ISBN 978-93-81904-86-2

Published in India by

Kalpana Shukla
KW Publishers Pvt Ltd
4676/21, First Floor, Ansari Road, Daryaganj, New Delhi 110002
Phone: +91.11.23263498/43528107
Email: knowledgeworld@vsnl.net • www.kwpub.com

Printed and Bound in India

Contents

Inward Foreign Investments in India and China:
A Comparative Perspective[1]

Abstract

Developing countries have increasingly received foreign direct investment (FDI) from developed countries starting from the second part of the last century. The pace has anything but increased in the present century. This flow has been aided by opening up of the economy by the developing countries through appropriate policies. The multinational corporations (MNCs) have taken this opportunity to expand to such countries to take advantage of the low cost base, large internal markets, reduced tariffs, abundant natural resources, etc. The developing countries on the other hand have benefited from the fund flows through acquisition of new technology, generation of employment, increase in productive capacity, increased competition leading to higher efficiency, increased production replacing imports hence leading to forex savings, etc. China and India being the major beneficiaries of FDI inflows have attracted a lot of attention among researchers and policymakers. It has been found that the FDI inflow in China is much more than that in India and the gap has constantly increased in favour of the former especially after the crisis year. This paper takes a fresh look at this divergence and tries to find out the reasons through simple correlation analysis (given dearth of post-crisis data points to carry out a regression analysis). It has been found that market size, economic development and trade flows might have caused the divergence in FDI inflows observed in recent years. For India, factors like deceleration of hi-tech exports to total exports, consumption expenditure, profit of FDI invested firms and services trade might have caused the flow of FDI to slow down in recent years. The policy of taxing domestic firms while giving incentives to FDI seems to have encouraged such flows into both the countries. Since taxes are lower in China and they treat FDI more favourably than India, this may have been the additional reason for the recent divergence in FDI inflows in these countries.

JEL Classification: F21

Key words: FDI, India, China

1. Introduction

Developing countries have increasingly received foreign direct investment (FDI) from developed countries starting from the second half of the last century. The pace has anything but increased in the present century. This flow has been aided by opening up of the economy by the developing countries through appropriate policies. The multinational corporations (MNCs) have taken this opportunity to expand to such countries to take advantage of the low cost base, large internal markets, reduced tariffs, abundant natural resources, etc. The developing countries on the other hand have benefited from the fund flows through acquisition of new technology, generation of employment, increase in productive capacity, increased competition leading to higher efficiency, increased production replacing imports hence leading to forex savings, etc. Debates regarding the beneficial effects of FDI, especially the ones coming to the extractive industries in developing and less developed countries, have pointed out to the absence of spillover effects to the host economies. Studies[3] related to FDI and impact on growth of the host countries did not find any conclusive evidence of positive relationship, especially in case of developing countries. In many of these studies the gravity model framework (Tinbergen, 1962) has been used to estimate these effects.

Many studies on FDI have also concentrated on the determinants of such flows both into and out of the countries. Factors like economic growth, exchange rate changes, and government policies, risks including political factors, exports, and imports have been found to be significant determinants of such flows. Among the developing countries China and India have been flushed with foreign capital from both developed countries and other emerging markets. Factoring out the differences in definition of FDI and accounting for phenomenon like round-tripping (discussed later) shows significant differences in level and growth of such flows in both the countries. The primary objective of this study is to find the determinants of the gap in level of FDI inflows in to India and China.

1.1 FDI in India

According to A. T. Kearney's 2007 Global Services Location Index India ranks second in the world in terms of financial attractiveness, people and skills availability and business environment. Until recently, the country's financial stability in the current environment of financial turbulence and a possible unwinding of macro imbalances sent a clear message to prospective foreign investors about India's position as an expanding investment destination. "India's external sector has displayed considerable strength and resilience since the reforms in 1991—despite several domestic as well as global political events and supply shocks in food and fuel . . . we partner with the global economy fully on the trade and current account while there is progressive liberalisation of the capital account, consistent with the progress in reforms in the real, fiscal and financial sectors," observed by Dr. Y. V. Reddy, former Governor of Reserve Bank of India (RBI) at the World Leaders Forum in New York some time ago. "The strong macroeconomic fundamentals, growing size of the economy and improving investment climate had attracted global corporations to invest in India. A major outcome of the economic reforms process aimed at opening up the economy and embracing globalisation has led to tremendous increase in Foreign Direct Investment inflows into India," he stated.

The Major benefits of Foreign Direct Investment (FDI) in case of India have been identified as filling the gap between investment funds required and domestic sources of funds. Technology transfer leading to knowledge diffusion and spillover effects on domestic firms. Transfer of superior organisational and management practices through links between the foreign investing company and the domestic firm (DIPP, 2004).

FDI policy in India has become increasingly liberal over the past half a century. In the first phase between 1969 and 1991 MRTP and FERA Acts restricted the operation of foreign firms in terms of size, type of products, equity participation, etc. In the second phase, during 1991 to 2000, FDI policy was substantially liberalised by allowing 51% foreign participation through automatic route in 35 high priority industries. During this period the Foreign Investment Promotion Board (FIPB) was constituted to consider FDI under the government route. The third phase, 2001 to the present, the FDI policy has been substantially liberalised with a negative list approach with all other activities permitted through the automatic route and substantial relaxation in terms of equity caps have also been made (ASSOCHAM 2012). Given the current scenario of historically low value of rupee against dollar the government is thinking of further relaxation of FDI norms.[4]

Figure 1: Sector-wise Automatic vs. Approval Route 1991 to 2010

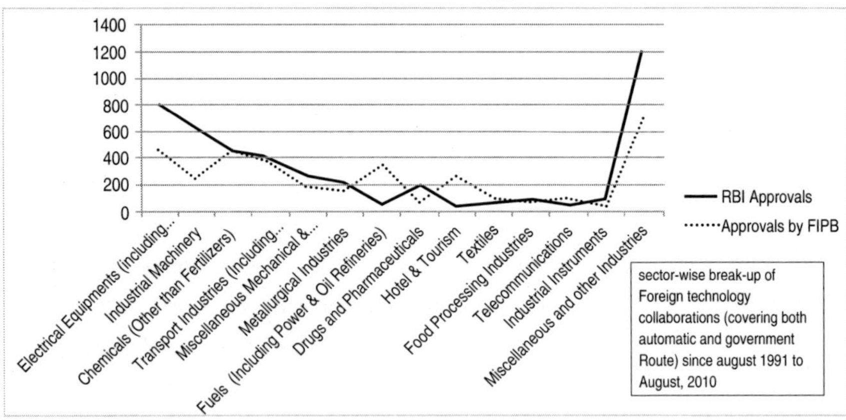

Source: DIPP Annual Report 2011

Figure 1 shows that for most of the sectors foreign technological collaboration through automatic route has surpassed that through approval route. This shows the impact of FDI policy liberalisation on technology collaborations. The number of investment proposals across states show that Chattisgarh has received the maximum in terms of magnitude, Rs. 1,045,645 crores between 1991 and 2010 which is around 13.72% of that received by all the states (DIPP, 2011). Almost 70% of the investments are in electricity and around 26% is in manufacturing (IBEF, 2010). This flows have been aided by enabling policy at the state-level and commensurate investment in infrastructure. Chattisgarh is closely followed by Orissa and Gujarat. In Orissa the major investments have happened in coal, thermal power and cement.[5] Gujarat on the other hand attracts most of the FDI in oil and gas, food processing, infrastructure and gems and jewellery among others.[6] Thus most of the FDI in high inflows recipient states have exploited the natural resource bases available in those locations. The following pie chart gives an overall view about regional distribution of foreign investment proposals.

Figure 2: Distribution of FDI Proposals across States/UTs 1991 to 2010

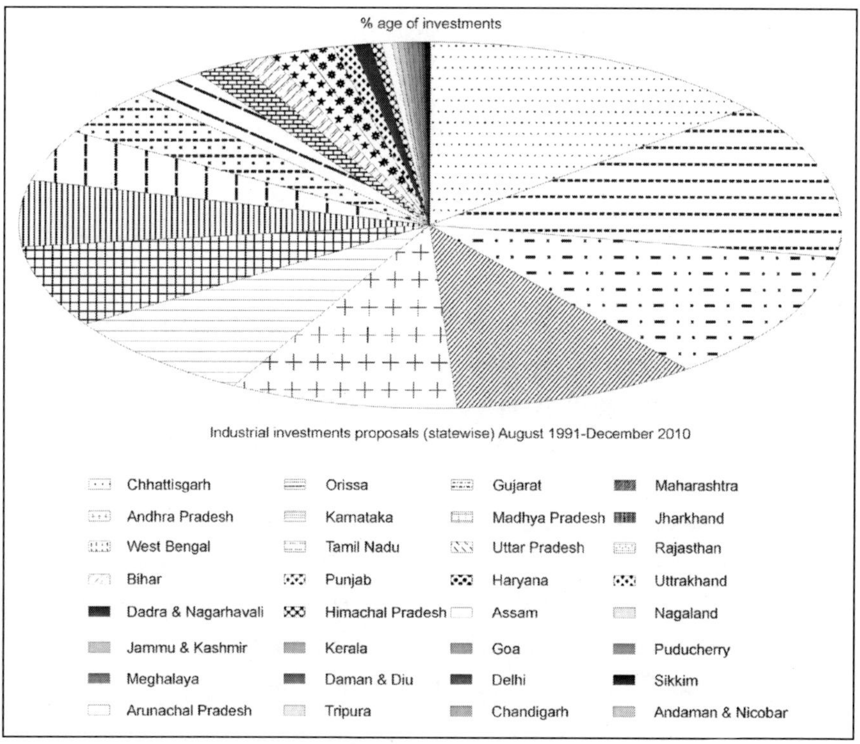

Sector-wise the bulk of the FDI proposals in the same period has come to electrical equipments and metallurgical industries. The following pie chart shows the sector-wise distribution of FDI proposals.

Figure 3: Distribution of FDI proposals Sector-wise 1991 to 2010

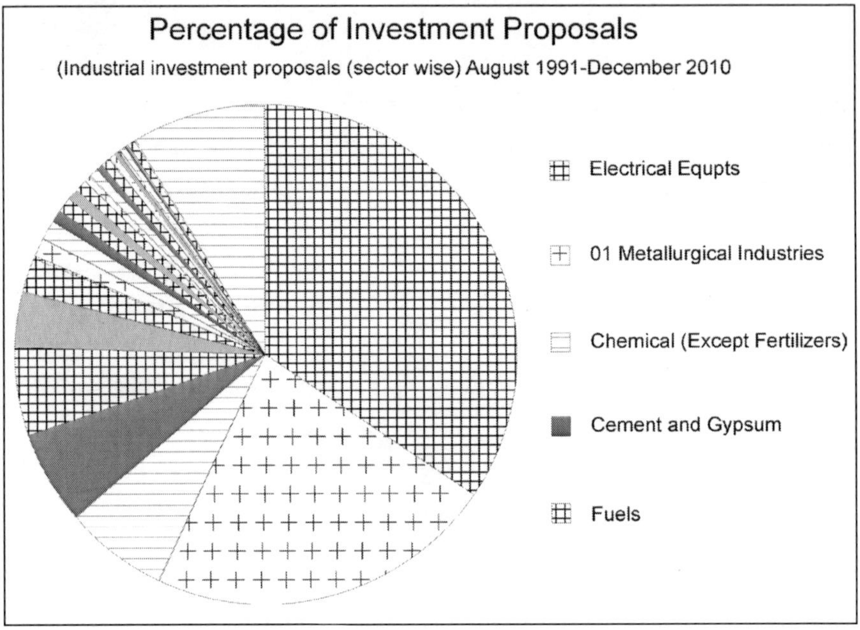

Data Source: DIPP

1.2 FDI in China

China can be cited as a successful example of transition to market determined economic system from a command economy. The economic reforms which had started in 1978 led to the acceleration of GDP to 10% annually similar to countries like Japan and Korea in their heydays. China has become the world's third largest economy, its number two exporter, and its leading manufacturer. Poverty rates have fallen to below 10% from the level of 50% at the beginning of the reforms process, with a substantial increase in the standard of living of its population. The reform process encouraged savings which laid the foundation for more investments. This led to the increase in productivity and facilitated movement of people from agriculture to manufacturing.

China embarked on the path of opening up at a much earlier stage than Japan or Korea did during early 1980s. The town and village enterprises (TVEs) operated at pre-reform procedures though they were operated in a different manner. Most of the changes happened under state ownership. Careful liberalisation was undertaken in key sectors though credit disbursement was closely conducted by the state.

In the beginning of the twentieth century a new development paradigm emerged, based on two principles. The first was that all business segments, private as well as others were allowed to compete on a level playing field in the market, other than sectors critical to national security or important otherwise. The second was that the state would regulate the economy mainly by forming, operationalising and applying rules for markets and their actors rather than directly controlling pricing and resource allocation. The development of this policy was caused by the accession to the World Trade Organisation in 2001. The constitutional amendment recognising the legality of private business and its role in the economy, enacted in 1999, was followed in 2004 by a further amendment openly mandating protection of private property.

Reform of regulatory institutions and practices had become a key theme of economic reform in the last decade. The major government restructuring done in 2003 marked a formal and decisive adoption of market-based regulation in place of economic planning, and included the integration of domestic and foreign economic policies into the government structure. In 2006, four key laws became effective. These included an advanced and better competition law that explicitly took into account key issues, including administrative abuse that had been inappropriately addressed by the previous anti-monopoly law; and a comprehensive bankruptcy law that drew on experiences of other countries. Amended company and securities laws also came into effect and proclaimed formal governance structures for joint-stock enterprises, rules for the issue and trading of securities on the exchanges, and rules to protect investors and minority shareholders. Key regulatory institutions were built or totally restructured and reformed. These include the China Bank Regulatory Commission, created in 2003 to regulate and supervise commercial banks and trust companies, the China Securities.

The Regulatory Commission was originally created in 1992 but acquired the major responsibility for all securities regulation in 2004, while the State Asset Supervisory and Administration Commission (SASAC), was established in 2003 to exercise the state's ownership in remaining SOEs. The authorities have made good use of international experiences and norms in formulating and implementing these reforms. The legal and regulatory reforms implemented over the years have already brought far-reaching and substantial benefits. Like, the reform and restructuring of the financial regulatory agencies have been instrumental in the success of efforts to restore the financial solvency of banks and securities companies, and to improve their governance and internal controls. These achievements provide the base necessary to allow financial institutions to diversify their services and products to adequately meet the economy's needs. The economic opening up and other reforms buoyed by China's WTO entry have spurred not only a boom in foreign trade and foreign direct investment (FDI), but also improved their quality. For example, China has become one of the largest exporters of information and communications equipment in the world, and its firms are moving beyond simple assembling of imported parts into processes requiring higher skilled labour and greater value-added technology inputs. The opening of the services sectors has already brought observable benefits, notably in distribution where the entry of several major international retail chains has helped to improve efficiency and lowered costs in the retail sector. Ultimately, the largest benefit from WTO is likely to result from its push to the broader economic reform process. The changes in laws and regulations prescribed by WTO on competition, intellectual property rights protection and other areas are as important and potentially beneficial to domestic businesses as to foreigners.

Figure 1 shows the movement in net FDI inflows into China between the years 1982 and 2010. Inflows have continuously increased over the period as can be observed from the positively sloped trend-line which has significant explanatory power (R^2=0.76). Regarding the sectoral shares it can be seen from the pie chart in Figure 2 that bulk of the FDI has flown to business activities. Among the manufacturing sectors electrical and electronic equipments have received highest FDI inflows followed by automobiles & transport equipment, and machinery & equipment.

Figure 1: Foreign Direct Investment, Net Inflows (BoP, current US$)

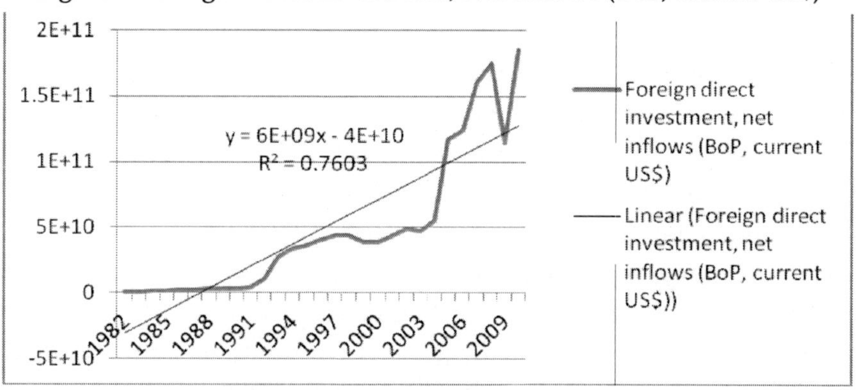

Source: UNCTAD Investment map

Figure 2: Average Sector-Wise Share of FDI 2001-10

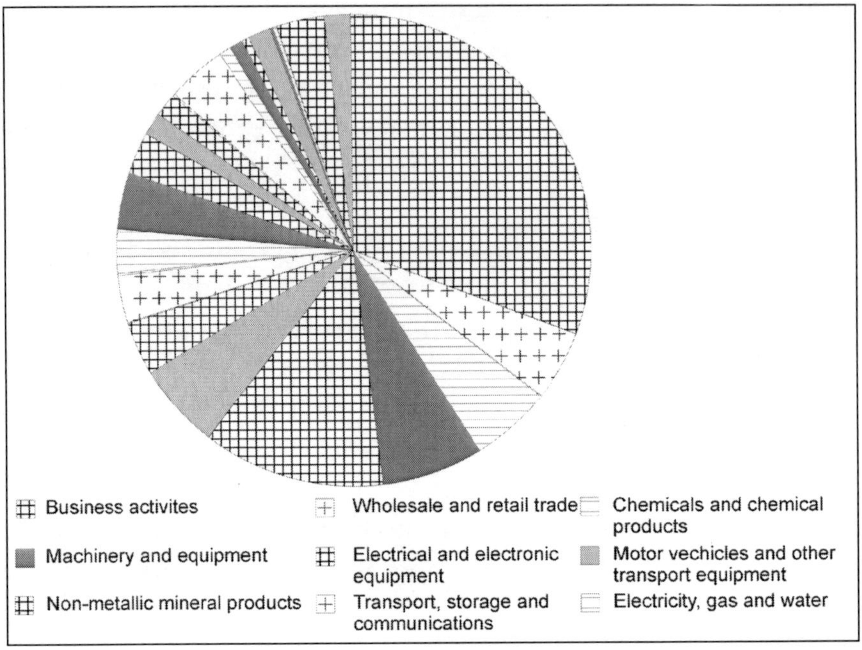

Source: UNCTAD Investment map

1.3 Comparison between India and China

In terms of FDI inflows it is observed that (Figure 3) the two countries were at the same level till 1990s but thereafter the gap widened till the year 2008 when the global financial Crisis occurred. The gap came down during 2009 because of the Crisis but strangely, continuously widened after that. Relative to market size, we have almost a similar scenario (Figure 4). The gap completely narrowed down during the Crisis and widened continuously thereafter. This is despite the fact that China (being more dependent on the external sector) was initially much more affected by the Crisis than India. Thus it would be interesting to find out the reasons behind such divergence after the Crisis. We would try to address this issue in this paper.

Figure 3: FDI Inflows in India and China

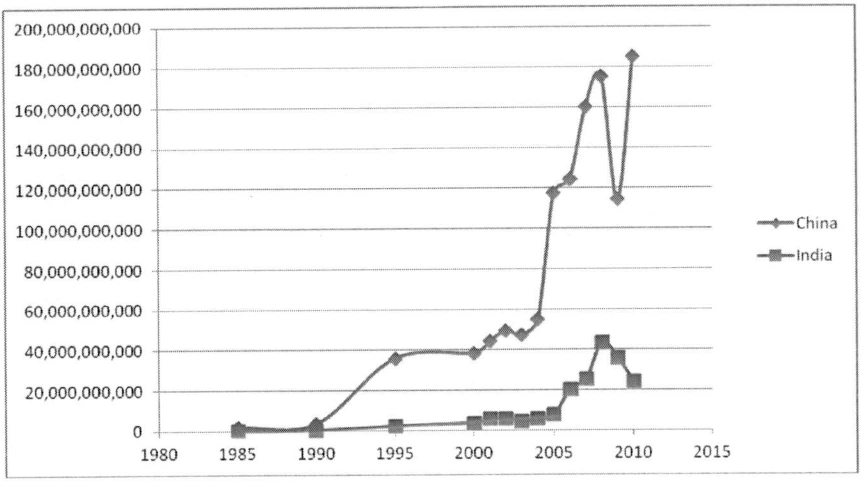

Data Source: UNCTAD Investment map

Bulk of the FDI inflows in China is from Hong Kong whereas in case of India it is from Mauritius. The Chinese diaspora present in Hong Kong is the main force behind investments in China. Chinese money rotated through "round-tripping"[7] (to take advantage of more favourable treatment of FDI) makes up for bulk of fund flows into the country. In the case of India the funds coming from Mauritius is from other countries routed through the latter due to Double Tax Avoidance Treaty (DTAA)[8] between these two countries. The common cause is the tax law favouring foreign investors which results in the maximum amount of flows to these two countries. This shows that tax policy plays a major role in determining FDI flows in these two countries. In the next section we discuss the theoretical issues related to cross-border capital flows which can explain the divergence in FDI flows into India and China.

Figure 4: FDI as a Percentage of GDP in India and China

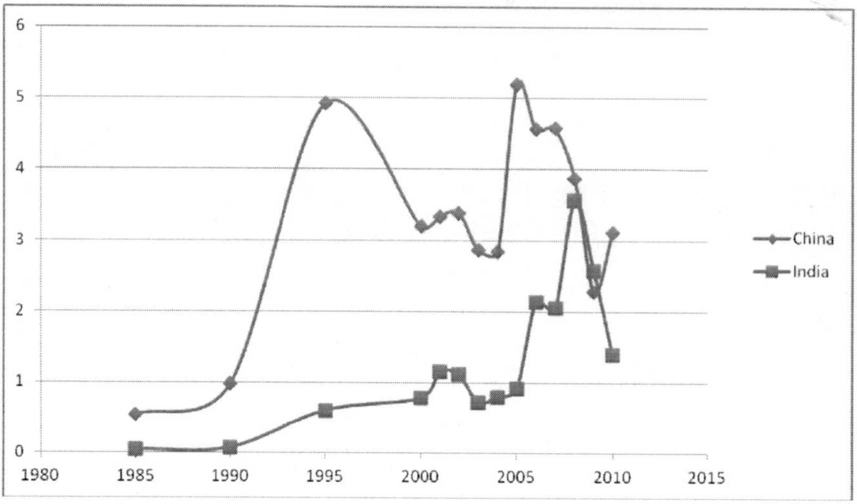

Data Source: UNCTAD Investment map

Table 1: Sources of FDI into India and China

China's FDI by source			India's FDI by source		
Source Country	2010	2011*	Source Country	2009-10 P	2010-11 P
Hong Kong	63.81	65.87	Mauritius	43.63564	37.59288
Taiwan	6.34	6.02	Singapore	9.874894	10.30859
Singapore	5.35	5.1	USA	9.848181	7.169155
Japan	4.01	5.72	Cyprus	7.225858	3.82221
USA	3.83	2.64	Japan	4.323049	8.407524
UK	2.55	1.5	Netherlands	3.579538	9.48524
ROK	1.55	2.25	United Kingdom	2.86274	3.601312
France	1.17	0.74	Germany	2.680201	1.091104
Netherlands	0.9	0.7	UAE	1.660656	1.258451
Germany	0.88	1.07	France	1.259962	3.25323
Others	9.6	8.4	Others	13.05819	14.01031

"P" means provisional figures

Source: DIPP, India and Columbia FDI Profiles for China

Section 2: FDI Inflows—Theoretical Underpinnings

The literature on determinants of FDI can be classified into firm-level, industry-level, macro-level partial equilibrium and general equilibrium approaches. A survey of all such studies can be found in Blonigen (2005). At the firm-level the most important determinant of establishing cross-border facilities is the profit motive where the surplus is higher from internalising the processes than from sourcing it from outside the firm (Rugman 1980, Dunning 2001). It is recognised that firm-level decisions are inherently unobservable and hence proxies like R&D intensity and advertisement intensity are used to understand the motives behind FDI. At the industry-level the motives are derived from studies at the firm-level. Karpaty and Poldahl (2006) survey the theories behind firm and industry-level determinants of FDI. They categorise the theories into asset exploiting, vertical and horizontal integration, strategic asset seeking and technology-sourcing types. Asset exploiting type has already been explained under firm-level determinants. Horizontal FDI (Markusen 1984) happens when trade costs are high whereas vertical FDI (Venables et al. 2004, and Dunning 1993) happens when the relative endowments of factors differ across countries and the MNE feels the urge to fragment the production process according to the location-specific advantages. Strategic asset seeking motive are found in oligopolistic markets for motives such as confronting the rival in their home market to creating concentration of market power[9] (Dunning 1993). In case of technology-sourcing motive the firm invests or acquires to gain knowledge about superior technology in the acquired firm (Kuemmerle, 1999; Griffith et al. 2003). Partial equilibrium macro-level studies consider market size, growth in market size, exchange rate, taxes, government policies towards FDI, trade barriers and quality of institutions as major determinants of FDI flows (Blonigen 2005). In the general equilibrium framework initially simple motives like horizontal and vertical integration (Markusen 1984 and Helpman 1984) have been modelled. Later studies concentrated on more complicated motives from using the host country as an "export platform" (Eckholm, Forslid, and Markusen, 2003, and Bergstrand and Egger, 2004) to using a number of locations as processors of intermediate goods which are shipped back to the parent country in more finished form (Baltagi, Egger and Pfaffermayr, 2004).

The theories can also be classified as "supply side" and "demand side." Supply side theories explain outward FDI depending on firm-characteristics. These are considered as external factors impacting FDI into certain countries (OLI paradigm). Contrasting to these theories we have "demand side" factors which are host country internal characteristics that attract FDI. As discussed above these are location-specific factors related to market size, growth, low cost resources, exchange rate movements, tax policy, tariffs, quality of institutions, etc. To explain the gap in FDI flows between China and India especially after the recession we would try to find the answers within these factors.

The other factor which merits a mention at this juncture relates to definition of FDI in both countries. The IMF definition includes around 12 items to constitute FDI.[10] China followed this definition while reporting their FDI figures whereas till 1999-2000 India only reported equity capital inflows as FDI. After a High-level Committee constituting RBI and DIPP endorsed following of IMF definition for measuring FDI, from 2000-01 India has reported these figures according to internationally accepted methods. Even after making such changes though, the gap in FDI inflows in these two countries has continuously increased (as we have discussed in Section 1).

Section 3: Past Studies

In one of the earliest studies on patterns of FDI inflows in India and China, Banik (2003) found the sequence of opening up the economies to be important determinant of such flows. Market size had a significant impact on FDI inflows in both the countries but had a higher coefficient for China. In the case of economic growth, on the other hand, India had a more significant coefficient than China. The other important determinants were investment rates for China and exchange rates for India. Thus flexibility of exchange rates helped FDI inflows into India whereas higher investment rates backed by higher savings rate caused complementary inflow of FDI into China.

One of the most comprehensive studies on the subject of FDI gap between India and China was carried out by Wei (2005). This Study identified comparability of statistics, differences in development strategies, differences in major economic indicators and overseas networks to be important determinants of the gap in FDI between India and China. The Study uses FDI into India and China from OECD countries to reduce the artificial difference in data of these two countries (due to "round-tripping" and difference in data definitions). They applied a decomposition method[11] to estimate the determinants of the FDI gap between the two countries. It was found that 50% of the difference can be explained by the larger market size and stronger international networks of China. On the other hand, lower labour cost, depreciating currency and stable economic and political environment in India was helping to close the gap.

Lane (2006) compares the international balance sheet position of India and China. The Study finds that India and China have a higher net foreign assets position than is warranted by their per capita incomes. In terms of composition of liabilities China and India have high holdings of dollars followed by yen for the former and significant holdings of pound sterling by the latter. In terms of equity flows portfolio investments are more significant in India, whereas in the case of China it is the FDI inflows. Empirical model estimation shows that market size is an important determinant of both debt and equity inflows in these two countries. In the case of FDI inflows into China total trade and distance are other significant determinants, whereas in the case of India movement of exchange rate with respect to that of partner countries was a significant determinant.

Comparison between intra-regional FDI flows into India and China shows that there is considerable regional disparity in these two countries. Siddharthan (2006) tried to find the determinants of the regional disparity in FDI inflows into India and China. He finds that per capita FDI inflows into the regions are significantly affected by per capita trade, social security expenditures, per capita income and freight costs at the regional level in China. In case of determinants of per capita FDI across Indian states he finds socio-economic development, education enrolment, percentage of urban population, per capita industrial output, tele-density and life expectancy at the regional level to be significant drivers.

Ranjan and Agrawal (2011) in one of the recent studies on the subject try to find the determinants of FDI inflows into BRIC (Brazil, Russia, India and China) countries. They find that market size, trade openness, labour cost, infrastructure facilities, macroeconomic stability and economic growth to be significant determinants of FDI inflows into BRIC countries.

The past studies thus have tried to explain the FDI inflows into India and China with respect to the economic, social and political indicators apart from data definition issues and overseas networks. In the next section we try to identify the reasons behind increase in FDI gap especially after the crisis year 2009. Since we do not have enough data points post 2009, a regression analysis would not be possible. We would try to find out the reasons through a simple correlation analysis of the relevant variables leaving a more in-depth analysis for future research when enough data points would be available.

Section 4: Explaining the recent divergence

As Table 2 shows in level terms China and India were almost at the same levels in terms of per capita income and exports in 1990. The gap has increased since then. In 2010 the per capita income level of China was almost four times that of India and exports almost seven times that of India. Thus economic development and external engagements may be important determinants of the divergence in FDI flows in recent years.

Table 2: Economic Determinants

	GDP per capita		*Export ($ mil)*		*Import ($ mil)*	
Year	**China**	**India**	**China**	**India**	**China**	**India**
1990	314	374	62,091	17,969	53,345	23,580
2000	949	453	249,203	42,379	225,024	51,523
2005	1,731	762	761,953	99,620	660,206	142,842
2007	2,651	1,105	1,217,790	149,951	956,233	228,686
2008	3,414	1,067	1,428,660	194,531	1,131,620	320,785
2009	3,749	1,192	1,201,790	164,921	1,004,170	257,187
2010	4,428	1,475	1,578,270	221,406	1,396,200	328,360

In terms of current a/c balance as a percentage of GDP China shows positive values whereas for India the value has been constantly negative. FDI inflows may be higher in a country with a positive balance since that shows comfortable foreign exchange position with lesser future risk. All other indicators ranging from literacy rate to internet users to crude steel output China is much ahead of India and differences have, if anything, increased over the years (Table 3).

Table 3: Other Economic Variables

Economic indicators	**1990**		**2000**		**2010**	
	China	**India**	**China**	**India**	**China**	**India**
% of Manufactured exports with high-technology		4	19	6	28	7
Current balance (% of GDP)	3	-2	2	-1	5	-3
Value added as % of GDP						
Agriculture	27	29	15	23	10	19
Industry	41	27	46	26	47	26
Services etc.	32	44	39	50	43	55
Selected economic indicator						
Lending interest rate	9.4	16.5	5.9	12.3	5.8	
Phone subscribers (per 100 people)	1	1	11	3	22	3

Adult illiteracy rate	78		91		94	
% Internet users of total population			1.7	0.5	31.6	8.5
Selected industrial output						
Crude steel (thousand metric tons)	66,349	14,963	128,500	26,924	626,654	68,321
Electricity (billion kwh)	621.204	289.438	1356.235	561.248	3695.928	899.389

Figure 5: Doing Business Rankings (the World Bank)

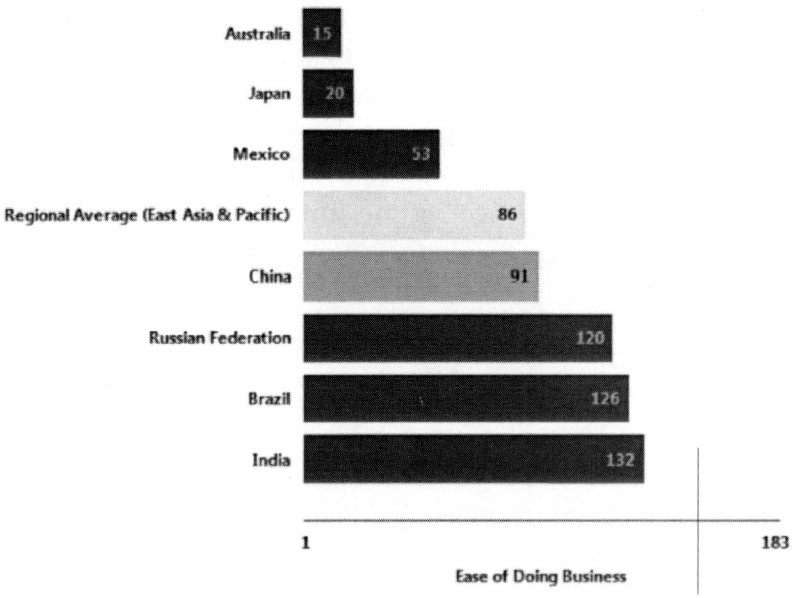

In terms of ease of doing business, though both the countries have low rankings, China is almost 40 ranks ahead of India in the 2012 Report (Figure 5). The major contributor to this difference is registering a property, resolving insolvency and enforcing contracts (Figure 6). China ranks much higher than India on all these three aspects. Strangely, though, in terms of economic freedom measures India is ahead of China (Table 4). It seems that FDI is more related to business related measures than quality of political institutions. China also has large natural resource endowments. In addition, China's physical infrastructure is more competitive, particularly in the coastal areas. But, India may have an advantage in technical manpower, particularly in information technology. China has a gigantic domestic market with a system of mass production. This reduces the cost of production considerably. Thus China is the first choice of multinationals for setting up a wholly export-oriented unit. India too offers an equally attractive environment. There is no dearth of technically qualified manpower available cheaper than in the West. But India has yet to evolve a system of bulk production at the scale prevalent in China.

Figure 6: Comparison of Doing Business Rankings

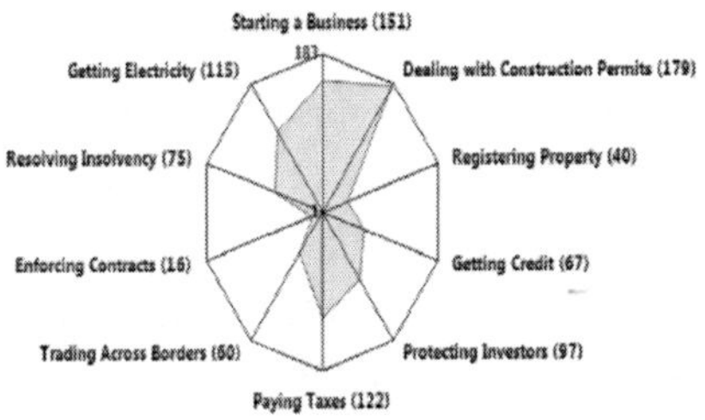

China

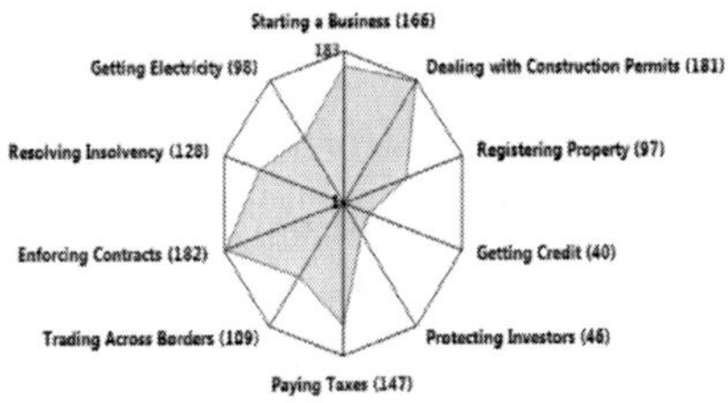

India

Table 4: Economic Freedom Comparisons

Index of economic freedom 2012		
Indicators	China	*India*
Property Rights	20	50
Freedom from corruption	35	33
Government Spending	84.1	74.8
Fiscal freedom	70.4	76.1
Business Freedom	46.4	35.5
Labour Freedom	55.4	74.2
Monetary Freedom	74.2	62.9
Trade Freedom	71.6	64.1
Investment Freedom	25	35
Financial Freedom	30	40
Overall Score	51.2	54.6
World Rank	138	123

Source: Economic Freedom Index, The Heritage Foundation, US

China has "more business-oriented" and more FDI-friendly policies than India. China's FDI procedures are easier, and decisions can be taken rapidly. China has more flexible labour laws, a better labour climate and better entry and exit procedures for business. Policies are geared more towards exports in China than in India. In terms of BITs (Bilateral Investment Treaties) China is much ahead of India. The country has signed 128 such treaties compared to 83 by India.

In terms of the general determinants of FDI inflows it is seen that correlation between GDP, GDP per capita in purchasing power parity terms (GDPCPP), goods exports (goodexp), goods imports (goodimp) magnitudes are large and positive in sign for both the countries but the coefficients are larger for China than India (Table 5). Thus market size, economic development and trade may have caused the divergence in FDI observed in recent years. For India correlation coefficients are higher for hi-tech exports to total exports (hitechtotexp), consumption expenditure, profit of FDI firms (profitFDI), openness (open) and services trade to total trade (tradsertgdp). In recent years on all this counts India is performing poorly. GDP growth has decelerated due to which factors dependent on it have also slowed down. Exports had slowed down due to the financial crisis affecting the demand originating from developed markets. This may have caused FDI flows to slow down in India in recent times.

Table 5: Correlations between FDI inflows and some important determinants

	China		India	
Factors	*FDI%GDP*	*FDI*	*FDI%GDP*	*FDI*
Export	0.263619	0.960631	0.619142	0.866485
GDP	0.064825	0.899793	0.566526	0.844354
GDPCPP	0.068299	0.900958	0.569575	0.846437
goodexp	0.238614	0.963786	0.620938	0.878957
goodimp	0.184127	0.945862	0.645164	0.893351
Hitechtotexp	0.415992	0.473617	0.540145	0.613597

Consumption expenditure	-0.08705	0.784798	0.622	0.877544
ProfitFDI	0.049551	0.884575	0.667042	0.909109
Royalty	0.047718	0.897577	0.490726	0.792121
Serexp	0.150414	0.946186	0.624369	0.881669
Serimp	0.075543	0.916881	0.547603	0.836137
Open	0.794457	0.510352	0.731089	0.876602
tradsertgdp	0.690001	0.482518	0.731602	0.89227

In terms of other determinants the correlations are high and negative between overall tariff and FDI inflows in both the countries with the magnitude being higher in China. Taxation of domestic firms seems to have encouraged FDI into India and China as they get favourable tax treatments in both the countries. Real Effective Exchange Rate (REER) seems to have little impact on FDI flows into the countries in recent times. Recent divergence in FDI inflows in these countries might have been caused by lower taxes and favorable treatment of FDI in China than India.

Table 6: Correlations with other variables

	Correlation	
	IndFDI	ChnFDI
Tariff	-0.8490601	-0.76033
Tax	0.71591794	0.737953
REER	-0.1232088	0.326028

Apart from these reasons a few other points merit a mention at this juncture. The policy towards FDI in multi-brand retail in India shows that government is hesitant about such flows in sensitive sectors. The situation is much better in China.[12] Moreover, the legal environment related to foreign firm operations in India was severely dented because of the ruling by the Supreme Court which cancelled all the 2G licenses granted on grounds of corruption. This caused resentment among the foreign investors[13] who had a considerable stake in the telecom sector. The exchange rate depreciation might be an additional factor in slowing down FDI flows in India due to its impact on cost of production (though correlations were not found to be significant between overall FDI and REER (Table 6)). Finally, the policy changes[14] in China towards enhancing domestic demand may have diverted FDI inflows which are market seeking towards this country away from India.

Section 5: Conclusion

In this paper we have tried to compare the FDI inflows in India and China and searched for the causes of increasing gap in such flows observed in recent years. We have come across a number of factors which may have caused such differences. From past studies, factors like difference in definition of FDI, round-tripping, development strategy, policies towards FDI, market size, economic growth, economic development, exports, tariffs, exchange rates, etc. have been cited as determinants of the gap. It has been observed that FDI inflows gap has increased in favour of China from the 1990s to 2008, and in 2009 it came down due to the global financial crisis. The flows strangely diverged thereafter with that increasing for China and decreasing for India.

We tried to find out the reasons for such divergence. Since we do not have enough data points to carry a pre-post kind of analysis we resort to simple correlations among important determinants and FDI flows in both the countries. Other reasons like policy and economic management in recent years have also been considered. In terms of the general determinants of FDI inflows, it is seen that correlation between GDP, GDP per capita in purchasing power parity terms, goods exports, goods imports correlations are very high positive for both the countries but the coefficients are higher for China than India. Thus differences in market size, economic development and trade may have caused the divergence in FDI observed in recent years. For India correlation coefficients are higher for hi-tech exports to total exports, consumption expenditure, profit of FDI firms, openness and services trade to total trade. In recent years on all these counts India is performing poorly. GDP growth has decelerated causing factors affected by it to slow down. Exports had slowed down due to financial crisis affecting the demand from developed markets. This may have caused export oriented FDI to come down in India in recent times.

The correlations are high and negative between overall tariff and FDI inflows in both the countries with the magnitude being higher in China. The negative relationship between tariffs and FDI shows that reduction of tariff barriers have encouraged FDI which is efficiency seeking (Goldar and Banga 2007). Policy of taxing the domestic firms while giving incentives to FDI seems to have encouraged such flows into both the countries. Real Effective Exchange Rate seems to have little impact on overall FDI flows into the countries. The recent fall in the value of rupee with respect to the dollar, and huge current account deficit, may cause further slowdown of FDI inflows into India. Since taxes are lower in China and they treat FDI more favorably than India these may have been additional reasons for such divergence.

The policy towards FDI in multi-brand retail, the legal environment related to foreign firm operations (ruling of Supreme Court which cancelled all the 2G licenses granted on grounds of corruption), the exchange rate depreciation in India and finally, the policy changes in China towards enhancing domestic demand may have diverted FDI inflows, which are market seeking, away from India.

References

Arindam Banik. 2003. "Foreign Direct Investment Inflows To India And China: Trends, Assessments And Determinants," Savings and Development, vol. 27, no. 1, 2003, 5-22.

Assocham. 2012. "India's Experience with FDI: Role of a Game Change." Report ASSOCHAM India.

Baltagi, Badi H., Peter Egger, and Michael Pfaffermayr. 2004. "Estimating Models of Complex FDI: Are There Third-Country Effects?" Mimeo.

Barbara-Navaretti, G. and Veneables et al. 2004. "Multinational Firms in the World Economy." Princeton University Press. Bergstrand, Jeffrey H. and Peter Egger. 2004. "A Theoretical and Empirical Model of International Trade and Foreign Direct Investment with Outsourcing: Part I, Developed Countries." Mimeo.

Blonigen, Bruce A. 2005. "A Review of the Empirical Literature on FDI Determinants." University of Oregon and NBER Initial Draft: December 2004. This Draft: April 2005 International Atlantic Economic Society session at the 2005 ASSA conference in Philadelphia, PA.

DIPP. 2004. OECD Back Paper, DIPP, GOI.

DIPP. 2011. Annual Report, DIPP, GOI.

Dunning, John H. 2001. "The Eclectic (OLI) Paradigm of International Production: Past, Present and Future." *International Journal of Economics and Business*, 8(2): 173-90.

Dunning, J. 1993. *Regions, Globalization, and the Knowledge-Based Economy.* Oxford University Press.

Dunning, J. H. 1993. *Multinational Enterprises and the Global Economy*. Addison-Wesley.

Ekholm, Karolina, Rikard Forslid and James R. Markusen. 2003. "Export-Platform Foreign Direct Investment," NBER Working Paper No. 9517.

Goldar, B. and R. Banga. 2007. "Impact of Trade Liberalization on Foreign Direct Investment in Indian Industries," Asia-Pacific Research and Training Network on Trade Working Paper Series, No. 36, June 2007.

Griffith, Rachel, Rupert Harrison, and John van Reenen. 2003. "Technology Sourcing by UK Manufacturing Firms: An Empirical Analysis Using Firm-level Patent Data," Working Paper, Institute of Fiscal Studies, London.

Helpman, Elhanan. 1984. "A Simple Theory of International Trade with Multinational Corporations," *Journal of Political Economy*, 92(3), 451-71.

IBEF. 2010. "Chattisgarh, Report on Investment Climate and FDI in Chattisgarh," IBEF, India.

IFC. 2012. "Doing Business in a more Transparent World," Doing Business Report 2012, IFC, The World Bank, Washington DC.

Karpaty and Poldahl. 2006. "The Determinants of FDI Flows Evidence from Swedish Manufacturing and Service Sector." Svenska Natvertet for Europaforskning i Ekonomi.

Kuemmerle, W. 1999. "Foreign Direct Investment in Industrial Research in the Pharmaceutical & Electronic Industries—Results from a Survey of Multinational Firms," *Research Policy*, 28, 2-3: 179-93.

Markusen, James R. 1984. "Multinationals, Multi-Plant Economies, and the Gains from Trade," *Journal of International Economics*, 16(3-4): 205-26.

OECD. 2009. "China: Defining the Boundary Between the Market And The State." OECD Reviews of Regulatory Reform, OECD.

Ozturk, I. 2007. "Foreign Direct Investment—Growth Nexus: A Review of the Recent Literature," *International Journal of Applied Econometrics and Quantitative Studies*, vol. 4, no. 2, 2007.

Lane, Philip R. 2006. "The International Balance Sheets of China and India," IIIS, Trinity College Dublin and CEPR Preliminary Draft, March 2006.

Ranjan and Agrawal. 2011. "FDI Inflow Determinants in BRIC countries: A Panel Data Analysis," *International Business Research*, vol. 4, no. 4, October 2011.

Rugman, Alan M. 1980. "Internalization as a General Theory of Foreign Direct Investment: A Re-Appraisal of the Literature," Weltwirtschaftliches Archiv, 116(2): 365-79.

Siddharthan. 2006. "Regional Differences in FDI Inflows: China—India Comparison," Institute of Economic Growth, Delhi University North Campus, Delhi 110007, India.

Tinbergen, J. 1962. "Shaping the World Economy," The Twentieth Century Fund, New York.

Wan, X. 2010. "A Literature Review on the Relationship between Foreign Direct Investment and Economic Growth," *International Business Research*, vol. 3 no. 1.

Wei, Wenhui. 2005. "China and India: Any Difference in Their FDI Performances?" *Journal of Asian Economics*, 16, 2005, 719-36.

Notes

1. Paper Presented at Conference on "Analysing the rise of India and China: Domestic, Regional and Global implications," Joint conference organised by "Institute of Foreign Policy Studies," University of Calcutta, "Centre for Contemporary India Research and Studies," Institute of International Relations, University of Warsaw and Global College International, Kathmandu in cooperation with Embassy of Poland in India (February 12-16, 2012).
2. Assistant Professor, Indian Institute of Foreign Trade, Kolkata Campus.
3. See Wan (2010) and Ozturk (2007) for survey of recent literature on FDI Growth nexus.
4. Raghuram Rajan, Chief Economic Adviser, Government of India, *The Financial Express*, June 12, 2013.
5. http://www.teamorissa.org/Investment%20Proposals%20Cleared%20till%2036th%20SLSWCA%20(%20as%20of%2031%20Dec%202010)_new.pdf.
6. http://business.mapsofindia.com/fdi-india/states/gujarat-economy.html.
7. Round-tripping can take many forms such as under-invoicing exports, over-invoicing imports, and overseas affiliates of Chinese companies borrowing funds or raising capital in the stock market and reinvesting them in China.
8. A large number of foreign institutional investors who trade on the Indian stock markets operate from Mauritius, and the second being from Singapore. According to the tax treaty between India and Mauritius, capital gains arising from the sale of shares are taxable in the country of residence of the shareholder and not in the country of residence of the company whose shares have been sold. Therefore, a company resident in Mauritius selling shares of an Indian company will not pay tax in India. Since there is no capital gains tax in Mauritius, the gain will escape tax altogether. The Finance Bill 2012 in India proposed that the residence certificate from origin country for tax exemptions would be necessary but not sufficient condition for getting benefit under DTAA. This created panic among investors from such countries, but the government later clarified that things have not changed and exemptions would be given.
9. Caterpillar, an earth-moving Machinery Company, entering Japan to confront its potential rival Komatsu which helped it sustain its market power for considerable amount of time. It delayed Komatsu's growth by ten years.
10. Equity capital, reinvested earnings of foreign companies, inter-company debt transactions, short-term and long-term loans, financial leasing, trade credits, grants, bonds, non-cash acquisition of equity, investment made by foreign venture capital investors, earnings data of indirectly held FDI enterprises and control premium, non-competition fee, and so on.

11. Oaxaca-Blinder decomposition of the gap.
12. When this Chapter was being written the Indian Government had given its endorsement to FDI in multi-brand retail on September 14, 2012 with some riders.
13. Telenor from Norway joint venture with Unitech, Etisalat from UAE joint venture with DB Realty felt like victims caught in a riot (*The Times of India*, February 2, 2012).
14. Like discouraging savings and encouraging consumption through reforms of tax rates and financial markets.